Who In The Heck Do You Think You Are?

A woman's guide to discovering the key benefits of self-awareness.

MICHELLE AAYE
www.michelleaaye.com

AFFILIATE DISCLAIMER. The short, direct, non-legal version is this: Some of the links in this book may be affiliate links which means that I earn money if you choose to buy from that vendor at some point in the near future. I do not choose which products and services to promote based upon which pay me the most, I choose based upon my decision of which I would recommend to a dear friend. You will never pay more for an item by clicking through my affiliate link, and, in fact, may pay less since I negotiate special offers for my readers that are not available elsewhere.

DISCLAIMER AND/OR LEGAL NOTICES: The information presented herein represents the view of the author as of the date of publication. Because of the rate with which conditions change, the author reserves the right to alter and update her opinion based on the new conditions. The book is for informational purposes only. While every attempt has been made to verify the information provided in this book, neither the author nor her affiliates/partners assume any responsibility for errors, inaccuracies or omissions. Any slights of people or organizations are unintentional. If advice concerning legal or related matters is needed, the services of a fully qualified professional should be sought. This book is not intended for use as a source of legal or accounting advice. You should be aware of any laws which govern business transactions or other business practices in your country and state. Any reference to any person or business whether living or dead is purely coincidental.

ISBN 978-1-7374637-0-2 Paperback

Cover Design: Thornton Online Marketing LLC

Table of Contents

Acknowledgements

God, I thank you for your love and patience with me. I thank you Lord for all the highs and lows that I have gone through over the years that lead to me breaking down so that YOU could build me back up. Getting to know you was the best decision of my life and I am grateful that I get to share you with other women that are where I was.... the fast track to self-destruction. Thank you for allowing me to see more and more of the ME that YOU made me to be daily. I love you Jesus!

Kourt and Ky, you all have been my riders from day one of me saying that I wanted to take on the world of loving other people.... No matter if it was doing stand-up comedy or ministry, YOU both were always there to say "mommy, you can do it!" You could have gotten off this ride a long time ago, but you stayed and I'm all the better for it! Thank you both for your unconditional love and support!
"Mommy loves you!"

I would also like to thank my family and friends for their support and motivation to complete this project. You guys helped me to live this book just by helping me live REAL LIFE. Thank you for accepting and believing in me when I sometimes doubted myself. I love you all.

And lastly, a special thank you to Mr. and Mrs. Hustle. Cortez I just don't have enough words to express my gratitude for not only being an awesome mentor but the best coach and manager/producer/publicist/encourager /lil brother ever! I am thankful for your obedience to God and your abundance of patience! You are one of the rare folks that God has enabled (as much as you are able to) see what HE has put in me. You not only see it, but you hold me accountable from that place! Mrs. Hustle.... A special S/O to you because it is what YOU do behind the scenes that allows Cortez to be all that God has called him to be. Thank you for being a phenomenal example of what a supportive, loving, make "IT" happen wife is supposed to be!

Preface

Who in the Heck Do You Think You Are was written from a place of love and a desire to help any woman who is struggling with an identity crisis in knowing who they are and more importantly who they are meant to be.

Ladies, I have lived this book! In every chapter you get REAL and TANGIBLE steps to deal with the things that may be preventing you from seeing yourself clearly in the mirror. You also get a little glimpse of how or what I might have encountered while dealing with the same thing. The road to knowing and loving YOU is not an easy quick destination. There is NO shortcut! However, it is the most worthwhile journey you will EVER take!

There are a few things that I will tell you upfront about this process, 1). You must be serious about *wanting* to become a better you and having a better life.

In short, YOU HAVE TO DO THE WORK TO GET OPTIMAL RESELTS. 2). You CANNOT do this without God (Jesus). As a matter of fact, getting to know God more intimately, not in a spooky spiritual way, but in real relationship way, is where you begin the journey. It is imperative that you know how and why He loves you. After this you need to know what He says about you. You must redefine your identity from who you think you are to who HE says you are.

My prayer is that this book will simply cause ladies to look in the mirror and desire a transformation to the next and best version of themselves. However, nothing can begin until you turn the next page!

Now let's do this!

Thank you for choosing to take this journey into discovering... *Who In The Heck Do You Think You Are?*

Before We Get Started

Did You Know?

Genesis 1:27 *~ "So God created mankind in his own image, in the image of God he created them; male and female he created them."*

Jeremiah 1:5 *~ "Before I formed you in the womb I knew you, before you were born I set you apart; I appointed you as a prophet to the nations."*

1 Peter 2:9 *~ "But you are a chosen people, a royal priesthood, a holy nation, God's special possession, that you may declare the praises of him who called you out of darkness into his wonderful light."*

Ephesians 2:10*~ "For we are God's handiwork, created in Christ Jesus to do good works, which God prepared in advance for us to do."*

INTRODUCTION

Getting to know yourself might seem more than a little boring. After all, what else is there to know? You've spent every second of your life with yourself.... So there certainly can't be any surprises, right?

Well, you're not alone if you feel this way, but you'd be wrong also!

You know a lot less about yourself than just about anyone else in your life knows about you.

Truth is, we don't see ourselves very well, and that's because we don't *really want* to look. We're afraid of what we'll find. We avoid examining ourselves daily. We'd rather turn on the TV, find a snack (my snack of choice-Moon Pies- Yumm!), or watch videos online. We are willing to do almost anything to avoid seeing THE TRUTH!

As unpleasant as the truth may be, it holds the secret to greater levels of success.
Understanding yourself is key.

When you understand yourself, you can:

- Gain control over yourself
- Avoid your weaknesses and common pitfalls
- Understand and deal with your negative habits
- Have healthier relationships
- Choose a life path that suits you well
- Find enthusiasm and happiness in the things you do

Big Picture: We're all suffering from a case of Mistaken Identity.

We've bought into the American dream like it's a one-size-fits-all solution. We have jobs we can't stand; while at the same time, we can't figure out what it is we'd rather do.

We repeat the same mistakes over and over, but don't have a clue we're doing it. On the off-chance we recognize our repeated mistakes, we don't understand why we're doing them or how to change it.

Success is much more challenging without self-knowledge.

You CAN Win.

To be highly successful, it's necessary to:

- Set big goals that are meaningful to you
- Utilize your strengths and avoid and or redirect your weaknesses
- Deal with stress in a productive manner
- Know how to motivate yourself
- Overcome fear
- Persevere

All these items are easier to accomplish if you know yourself. Without self-knowledge, luck becomes main factor here. And I'm sure we all know "Luck" only counts when pitching horseshoes! Lol!

Remember Me Quote:

"Luck is for the Unprepared"
-Karen Lynch

Notes:

DISCOVER YOUR TRUE SELF

Psalm 139:14-16

14 I praise you because I am fearfully and wonderfully made;
your works are wonderful,
I know that full well.
15 My frame was not hidden from you
when I was made in the secret place,
when I was woven together in the depths of the earth.
16 Your eyes saw my unformed body;
all the days ordained for me were written in your book
before one of them came to be.

"I used to be terrified of being my true self. Like many young girls and a lot of adult women, I didn't have the self-confidence, self- esteem or belief that anyone would or could like the REAL ME, so I tried to stay hidden as much as possible. However, what I didn't realize was, that the real me was in fact still IN me, showing...like a slip hanging just below the hem line of your favorite dress....

Like a mis tucked shirt-tail, Like the tag on that new blouse you just bought ***and wore*** *that you intend to return; I was peeking out trying to be unnoticed but I was still there, all along... regardless of how I tried to hide. But one day I finally discovered, that in THOSE moments... those poorly hidden, peek-a-boo, awkward moments... that I was actually at my BEST! It was then that I began to embrace who I was. Then something wonderful happened when I did this, others began to embrace me too!"*
~Michelle Aaye

Your true self-is the part of you that's constant. It's the part of you that you would recognize, even if you had been brought up in another country and had a totally different set of experiences. It's the part of you that makes you uniquely you. **Over the years, we often lose sight of this person.**

It's the unadulterated you. It's the person you would be if you were free from worry about the opinions of others. It's the 100% real deal baby! It's the you without any **fear or doubt**.

Let's Dive In:

Discover your true self that's lurking beneath the surface of your fear and erroneous beliefs:

1. **What would my dream profession be if I knew I would be successful, and no one would judge me negatively?** Do you dream of being a musician, but you've chosen to be an accountant? You're probably more a rock star at heart, I bet.

    - Somewhere along the way, you've allowed yourself to believe you were less capable than you really are.

- Knowing your dream profession tells you a lot about yourself.

- What does your dream profession tell you about you? How close does your current career come to delivering the same experience? (Be Honest!)

2. **Whom do I most or least admire?** You can learn a lot about yourself by the people you admire or feel disgusted by. Who are some people in your life or from history that you admire? Which people turn your stomach? (Be prepared, your own answers may shock you!)

    - What does this tell you about yourself?

3. **What are my greatest accomplishments? This is a way of learning what you value.** What have you done that you're most proud of? Why do those things make you feel good? (Time to Celebrate you!)

4. **What are you ashamed of?** What have you done that you regret? What things from your past would you prefer to keep a secret? What can you learn about yourself from the fact that you feel shame about them? (*TIP: Once identified, **YOU MUST** Let It Go!*)

Your true self is that part of you that is constant from situation to situation. **No matter what you learn or experience, your true self stays the same.** The true self is hidden by our fears, our incorrect beliefs, and our concern of the opinions of others.

Values

What are your values? If you have to think for more than three seconds, you don't know them well enough to be highly successful. Our values determine what activities and ideals are most important to us. Choosing goals that violate your values is not only unwise and mentally unhealthy, but it also guarantees that in most situations you'll struggle, and most likely fail.

Living according to your values is beneficial to your self-esteem and your peace of mind. It's easier to achieve success when you're pleased with yourself!

Knowing your values is a MAJOR part of knowing yourself.

Remember Me Quote:

"Self-Awareness is NOT Self-Judgement; It is Looking and Seeing and Discovering who you really are.... So Check Judgement at the Door!"
-Unknown

Let's Dive In:

Try these techniques to discover your values:

1. **Make a list of every positive value you can think of.** This ***isn't*** about what others value. What do YOU think are positive values or qualities a person can have?

2. **Imagine you could only have 10 of these values.** What values would you choose for yourself? Which values would make you feel proud of yourself if you possessed them?

3. **Place those 10 values in order from most important to least.** It might be challenging but prioritize that list. What are the first three values? Does the life you're currently living reflect these values? Why not? (Be Honest)**The values you most admire are the values of your true self.** If you're miserable in your life, you're probably not living a life that exemplifies those values. Your success will be greatly limited if you're not living those values.

Based on the life you're living, what would you say your values are? If a stranger watched you for a week, what would they list as your three most important values?

Is there a discrepancy? If so, why?

Strengths and Weaknesses

Ok people... quick question: What is your momma's biggest weakness? (*Not going there, Barbara Jean would buss my head to the white meat from beyond the grave! Lol!)* How does your friend mess up every relationship she's ever been in? (*SHHHHH! Hush Nah! That was a rhetorical question*).

You can probably answer those questions without even thinking. Of course you can, figuring out other people's mess is always easier than figuring out your own!

Now, it's your turn in the spotlight! What is YOUR greatest weakness? What do YOU need to change in order to be much more successful? Do YOU know? Even if you have an answer, ask a few of your friends for their honest opinion as well. Also, ask someone you only know casually.

You'll likely find that everyone's answers agree, except for your own. You might not like their answers, but down deep, if they all align, you'll know they're correct.

We're pretty good at identifying our strengths. We like those! Our weaknesses on the other hand?? Not so much. We instinctively avoid our weaknesses, but we're not as consciously aware of them as we could or should be.

Ask yourself these questions to learn and leverage your strengths:

1. **What am I naturally good at?** What are some things that you seem to be better at than just about anyone else you know? **We all have at least a talent or two that most others seem to be lacking.** Make a list of these natural strengths. (Now is the time to brag on yourself girl... don't hold back!)

2. **What have I learned to be good at?** These are things that you have a lot of experience and interest in doing. While these might not be innate strengths, you've developed these skills into strengths. List these, too. (Don't be modest... no time for that! You Need to see your AWESOMENESS!)

3. **What do my friends and family view as my strengths?** Ask your friends and family to name some of your strengths. Push them to be honest with you. You're bound to hear a few things that surprise you. Add these to your list.

4. **What do other people compliment me for?** Are you complimented for certain things more often than others? Write these down, too.

5. **What are my favorite hobbies?** What do you love to do? Our hobbies are a demonstration of what we love to do or have a high level of interest in.

6. **What activities cause me to lose track of time?** What are the things you love to do so much that you can't believe how much time has passed when you look at the clock?

It's important to identify your strengths and interests. It's easier to be successful when you use your strengths and interests to your advantage. That only makes the best sense.

It's just as important to identify your weaknesses. Weaknesses either need to be remedied or avoided.

Imagine taking a long trip, and you know that there's a section of road along your journey that was washed out last month. You'd either ensure that it was repaired, or you would avoid that road.

Ok ladies, let me make it a lil more real for you! Imagine you go to the nail salon for a pedicure and low and behold they tell you your favorite nail tech, "Amy" is no longer working at the salon, so you get stuck with the new girl, "*AMY*" (what are the odds). But new "AMY" apparently is fresh out of nail school cause she is digging waaay to deep for the cuticle on your big toe and has got you singing Tamala Mann's, "Take Me to The King"! You ultimately leave the shop feeling like you need to throw yo whole foot away and start over!

Fast forward....time for your next pedicure and the only person available to take you is new "AMY"! Wouldn't you throw a hissy fit until the owner stops what he's doing and does your feet personally? (let's face it leaving is not an option, so you have to clown, it's summer outside!) Get my point now? You're not walking into that weakness! Lol!

Sorry, the point I was trying to make was this:

You might be surprised to discover that you've done a better job of hiding your weaknesses from yourself than you realize!

Let's Dive In:

These questions will help you understand your weaknesses:

1. **What are somethings that nearly everyone seems better at than I am?** There are things you're naturally gifted at, and others that are more challenging for you than for others. It's important to know what these things are. (This may be tough to do but you can do it!)

    - Start a new list for your weaknesses.

2. **What do I find challenging to learn or improve at?** Your serious weaknesses are those things you naturally struggle with, and you also struggle to learn. It's like a double whammy. **Don't worry, everyone has a few of these.** Identify these things and add them

to your list.

3. **What do my friends and family view as my weaknesses?** It will be challenging to get your friends and family to be honest on this one, but it's one of the most important things to know about yourself.

    - Push your friends and family to be honest. Give them the courtesy of not being offended by their opinions and insight.

4. **What hobbies or careers would I despise?** What are some hobbies you can't imagine doing? Hunting? Bowling? Playing cards? Needlepoint? Woodworking? What do the things you hate say about you?

- **The things you dislike may reveal weaknesses, too.** If you can't get yourself to do them easily, they're a weakness.

- Look for similarities between the things you dislike. What is the common thread?

5. **What activities make me miserable and drain my energy?** This is a little more specific than the previous question, but along the same lines. Some examples:

    - Maybe you can't stand attending parties or other social events.
    - Do you dislike spending time in the outdoors?
    - Sports?
    - Cultural activities?
    - Meeting new people?
    - Going to church?

6. **What are five careers that sound like pure torture to you?** Accounting? Sales? Artist? Medicine?

    - **What do the careers you dislike have in common?** Do you dislike them because every day is the same? Or, is it because they require talking to strangers?

    - What skills are needed to be good at those careers? Are you lacking in those skills?

Learn your weaknesses and understand them. **Self-knowledge regarding your weaknesses is critical to success.** Otherwise, it's like walking into a bear trap when you pursue a big goal. Go around the traps or disarm them by fortifying your weaknesses.

Remember, there's always someone else that's great in the areas you struggle. Success doesn't have to be a solo journey.

Notes:

REPEATING MISTAKES

Proverbs 24:16
16 for though the righteous fall seven times, they rise again,
but the wicked stumble when calamity strikes.

"Any lesson not learned is soon to be repeated... and Repeated... and REPEATED!" ref: George Santayana
"Life is full of lessons; good, bad, right, wrong and indifferent! One way or the other we WILL learn. Having the courage to self-examine can only help us in navigating successfully in these lessons. The sooner we "get it", the sooner we can move on to the next thing that life has for us. ***Spoiler Alert****: There will more than like be another lesson once we get there too!"*
~Michelle Aaye

It's not the occasional big mistake that derails your life and your efforts for success. It's the habitual mistakes you make. These are the mistakes you make over and over again. You can see these in other people from a mile away. They're much more challenging to notice in yourself.

We often view these as areas of our lives where we frequently suffer from "bad luck". Luck, good and bad, is evenly distributed across humanity. If you have an area of your life where you seem to be unlucky consistently, you're making one or more mistakes repeatedly.

This is going to take some soul searching and help from your friends and family. (Really Be Honest with yourself!)

Let's Dive In:

Analyzing these areas of your life can help you avoid making the same mistakes over and over:

1. **Review your life from beginning to end.** Look at your life sequentially and examine the times your life became miserable or chaotic. Look at the times you failed. What happened just before these situations occurred?

    - What did you do or fail to do?
    - What were you thinking at the time?
    - Where did you go wrong?
    - Do you see any patterns of incorrect action or thinking?
    - What would have been a better course of action on your part?

2. **Relationships.** Look back on your failed friendships and romantic relationships. Include your relationships with your family members, too.

    - Think back on every major disagreement you've had. What was your contribution to the cause?

    - Consider all of your relationships that have ended. How did you contribute to that relationship's end?

    - Examine your romantic relationships specifically. What do all of those people have in common? Are you choosing the wrong type of person for you?

- Ask your friends and family why they think your relationships failed.

3. **Finances.** Look back on your financial challenges. What led up to those challenges? Could you have done something differently to avoid them?

4. **Health.** What are the mistakes you're consistently making regarding your health? Are you going to the doctor regularly? Eating habits? Exercise? What mistakes are you making each day that keep your health and fitness less than acceptable?

5. **Work.** What are the mistakes you're making at work? Ask your coworkers and boss for advice on what you can do to improve. You'll be surprised by what you hear. (Warning what your told may be hard to hear. Remember if all the answers align, you've got some work to do)

The mistakes we make repeatedly are the biggest of anchors. **They sabotage us continuously, and in many cases, we are unaware of them.** Discovering and fixing these mistakes is a huge step toward finding greater success.

Notes:

MEDITATION - HOW DOES YOUR MIND WORK?

2 Corinthians 10:5

5 Casting down arguments and every high thing that exalts itself against the knowledge of God, bringing every thought into captivity to the obedience of Christ,

The mind can be an overly complex subject, however, learning about "how" our minds allow us to do what we do (or not do, in some cases) is pivotal. Once I began to understand how certain people think and process information, it was absolutely freeing. I stopped taking things so personal. If we are not careful with our minds in the way that we use them, we can find ourselves creating narratives that do not exist, creating stories that never happened or just seem down-right crazy to those around us.

We have to be intentional with our thoughts. We must be selective about what we see and hear as most thoughts are derived from what goes on around us.

~Michelle Aaye

Our minds are very different than they appear to be. There's the real world, and then there's what's going on between our ears. We all have a different view of the world. The thoughts and noise going on in our heads taint our perceptions. It's not easy to see the world and life without these filters changing our perspective in some way.

Meditation is one way to notice the activity and bias of our mind. It's also a great way to give your mind a well-deserved rest. Meditation provides a mental reset like nothing else!

Your mind is ultimately running the show. You can only apply so much willpower before you're out of gas. Understanding how your individual mind works is important.

Start a daily meditation practice. **You only need 15-30 minutes each day to get significant benefits.** There's a plethora of information to help you get started, from books to videos to guided meditations.

Notes:

DISCOMFORT AND YOU

Philippians 4:12-13

[12] I know how to [a]be abased, and I know how to [b]abound. Everywhere and in all things I have learned both to be full and to be hungry, both to abound and to suffer need. [13] I can do all things through [c]Christ who strengthens me.

We have all heard the saying, "Life is full of ups and downs". Now who doesn't like the ups of life, right? I mean, "when it's up, then it's up" (S/O to Cardi!) But it's those darn downs that no one likes! That's because what we often do is loose focus on the benefits of "the downs" when they do happen. Though they are not a real crowd pleaser, in most cases, "the downs" in life help us to grow in one way or another. They don't feel good, but we have to learn to see the silver lining in these situations.

When I lost my mother to Cancer 6 years ago, it was undoubtably the toughest thing I had ever had to deal with in my life! In that moment there was NO silver lining! Hell, I would have even settled for an old rusty one if I could have got one! I could not see anything good about life back then, or at least that what I thought. While she was in hospice there was soooo much to get done.

Praying with and for my mom, even when she had given up...being her part time caretaker, making sure her and my dad's bills stayed paid, figuring out who would care for my adult disable nephew they had custody of... seeing to my teenage daughters all this while managing one of the busiest depts at work, ***Talk about uncomfortable!***

What could I have possibly learned or gained during all this? Well, I learned that there was a lot more patience in me than I ever knew. I learned that when needed I was pretty darn good at time management (one of my all-time struggles) after all. And most importantly, I got valuable time with my mother that not many others did!

In those moments, our laughs were more authentic and purer and our "I love yous" seemed to linger in the atmosphere just a bit longer than normal. I was probably the closest I had ever been to my mom the last 9 months of her life than I had ever been in 44 years of my own.

My lesson from this extreme discomfort...Silver linings exist in all situations; you just have to have eyes to see them. Sure, it was not easy, and I did cry and pray a lot but somehow I came out of this tough time better than I was when it began.

~Michelle Aaye

Everyone has their pet methods for dealing with discomfort. Some are relatively harmless, while others can be quite destructive. It's possible to have strategies for dealing with discomfort that are actually beneficial!

The ways you deal with discomfort can either aid or detract you from your success.

Let's Dive In:

How do you deal with discomfort? Let's talk about it:

1. **What are you likely to do when faced with a task you don't feel like doing?** Imagine you know that you need to clean the garage, but you'd rather eat a bag full of nails instead. What are you likely to do?

    - Find another activity that needs to be done, but is more agreeable to you?

- Distract yourself in some way? What would you do instead?
- Take a nap?

Rationalize that it can wait until tomorrow?

- Make a plan to clean the garage in smaller chunks?
- Psych yourself up so you can get it done?

2. **How do you handle boredom?** If you have nothing to do, what are you likely to do?

- Choose a goal and work on it?
- Watch TV?
- Eat something tasty?
- Call or Text a friend?
- Take to Social Media?

3. **What is your response to stress?** You're feeling anxious or under pressure. How do you handle it? Do you drink? Eat? Sleep? Or do you find a way to relax and get things accomplished in your life?

4. **What are your bad habits? All negative habits provide one benefit: they make you feel better in the short-term.**

   They have no other benefits. Bad habits are ways of dealing with negative emotions. If we were "tough enough," none of us would have bad habits.

How do you deal with discomfort? The answer to this question tells you a lot. Poor responses to discomfort make life more challenging and decrease the odds of success. Handling discomfort appropriately gives you a huge advantage over the many people that do not.

There are better ways to deal with discomfort:

1. **Find a solution that works.** Imagine how powerful you would be if you immediately started looking for solutions to a challenge instead of looking for a distraction. (Period!)

2. **Relax.** This doesn't mean take a nap. **This means finding ways to reduce your discomfort enough that you can take action. Prayer and Meditation** are a couple of examples. Calling a friend is another.

3. **Exercise.** You'll reduce your stress and enhance your health. At least it isn't causing any harm or wasting time like the traditional responses to stress.

4. **Have a glass of really cold water.** It will snap you out of your mental state, and you probably need to drink more water anyway. (A reminder from EVERYONE's Mother!)

5. **Have a staring contest with your discomfort.** When you're uncomfortable, it won't last if you'll look it right in the eye.

    - Instead of doing something harmful or worthless, just sit with your discomfort and observe it.

    - How does it feel?

    - Where is it located in your body?

    - **Relax, keep watching it, and it will fade away.**

Discomfort is your mind's way of protecting you. This is great if you're about to risk your life, but it's misguided the majority of the time. Success is heavily dependent on the ability to overcome this discomfort and take appropriate action.

Become aware of how you handle discomfort and devise positive ways of handing these situations.

Notes:

HABITS

James 1:12

[12] Blessed is the man who endures temptation; for when he has been approved, he will receive the crown of life which the Lord has promised to those who love Him.

The things we do today help to create the things we will do in the future. Good or Bad, the habits we have now do ultimately affect our goals. When I think of all the habit's I've had over the years that I have actually stuck with, I can name very few that have actually aligned with my future goals and or my purpose. The habits I did have were simple, fruitless habits that were leading me nowhere. Habits like: My "tennis shoe" habit- I made sure I bought new tennis shoes each time I got paid. Then there was my buy a new wig each week habit. Then there was the see if the same people are REALLY at the club each week habit!

My point is, even though I looked good and was fairly sociable... the things I was creating as habits did not play a direct part into developing my skills towards my purpose. Intentionally engage in habits that will further your future goals.
~Michelle Aaye

Your habits control your destiny. It's not the amazing things you do or fail to do once a year that make a big difference. It's the things you do day after day that add up over time.

For example, think about how much brushing your teeth each day matters. Each individual day means nothing, whether you do it or not. But look at the difference between brushing your teeth every day for three years versus not brushing them at all for three years.

The difference is alarming! (*Note: Please don't try this example for real!*)

Many of the things you do, or don't do, regularly have a monumental impact on your success and failure.

We are aware of some of our habits, but not all of them. The previous section on how you handle discomfort exposed some of your habits, but there are more.

The key to increasing the odds of being successful is creating goals that are aligned with your purpose and values, and then creating habits that bring you closer to those goals. So, do your habits support your goals?

Let's Dive In:

Consider how your habits can make or break your odds for success:

1. **What is your morning routine?** Even if your morning routine was never planned, you've developed a routine. The question is whether or not it supports being successful.

    - What time do you wake up? Is that the best time to wake up to achieve your goals?

    - What do you have for breakfast? Does that support your health and alertness?

    - What do you think about in the shower?

    - Do you review your plan for the day?

- Do you review your goals?

- Do you give yourself enough time to arrive at work on time?

- What do you actually do each morning? What could you improve?

2. **What do you do for the first two hours at work?** The first couple of hours at work set the stage for the rest of the day. How do you use them?

    - Do you grab a coffee, gossip with your office biddies, and watch the episode you missed from Love & Hip Hop on the company computer?

- How do you spend this time, and is it the best way to support your career goals? (Think about it seriously)

3. **What is your routine when you get home from work?** Most of us change clothes and hit the couch or the dinner table. How do you spend the time? If you wait for the weekend to do anything worthwhile, you're only using two days of each week. Is that enough to be successful?

    - **What could you be doing each night to make the biggest difference in your life?**

4. **What is your routine during the last two hours of the evening?** How do you wind down from a long day?

- Do you learn something new each night?
- Review your goals?
- Take action toward your goals?
- Do you prepare for tomorrow?
- Do you waste your time?
- How do you spend your time? Are you spending it wisely?

5. **How do you spend your weekends?** Most of us have more flexibility on the weekends. Unfortunately, for most of us that means doing nothing worthwhile for the majority of the weekend. What habits do you have for the weekend? What habits would suit you better?

Understand your habits and how they impact your success. Poor habits lead to poor results. **The right habits create billionaires and other super successful people.**

Take a look at your current habits and think about the future you can expect.

Notes:

HOW TO FIND YOUR PASSION

Jeremiah 29:11

11 For I know what I have planned for you,' says the LORD.[a] 'I have plans to prosper you, not to harm you. I have plans to give you[b] a future filled with hope.

I have always been attracted to the idea of working in Television and or Radio. I remember being about 8 or 9 yrs old and telling my mom that I wanted to be a Television Talk Show Host. Now, I'm not talking Ophra or Steve Harvey... Jimmy Fallon or Stephen Colbert (although he is my fav right now!). I am talking Merv Griffin and Johnny Carson. Straight old school.... Well , old school to a kid that grew up in the '90's. Sadly though I let my mother convince me that I didn't really want that.

Back then she told me that they didn't put "people that looked like us" on tv! Whao! Imagine my surprise! I had to quickly educate her on how there were shows like The Jefferson's" and "What's Happening" that featured all black casts so yes indeed they DID put people like us on tv, mom!

Though I was feeling quite proud of myself in the moment, I learned ... that was not what she meant. She was referring to my size! Because I was a chunkier child, she did not believe that society, even back in the late 70's & 80's would be willing to accept an overweight person on television. Of course, we KNOW this is not true now... and I also knew it not true then either.

What I later learned was that my mom, who was also a chucky child/teen had tried to break into the music business with a singing group back in the late 50's and early 60's , however, and her peers were not accepting or kind to her.

Still having memories and fears from that experience, she inadvertently passed those to me by saying what she said. I don't believe for one moment my mom didn't want me to succeed or that she didn't believe in me. I believe her fear was stronger than anything else at that time and she didn't want me to go through what she did. I wish my momma was still here so that she could see me face, what she couldn't....
~Michelle Aaye

When you were a child, you were passionate about a particular career. The market may have tanked for becoming a cowboy or a dragon slayer, but you also lost your way. You allowed people to change your mind. Or you may have gotten a little lazy. Maybe you were more interested in impressing others than following your dream.

It's not too late to rekindle your passion. You know more about yourself now than you did when you were 18. It might be the perfect time to track down a compelling future.

We've talked around this topic by looking at your strengths, hobbies, values, and the people you most admire. Now, it's time to be more direct.

Goals and aspirations that include your passion are the easiest to attain.

Let's Dive In:

Ponder these questions and answer them truthfully. Your thoughts and answers will lead you to your passions:

1. **If you were the last person left on Earth, what would you want to do or learn?** Imagine you have access to every modern convenience. How would you choose to spend your time?

- This is an interesting question, because it eliminates the opinions of others. There is no one to impress or disappoint. It's just your interests and you.

- What would you want to learn? Many times, we want to learn something because of the benefit we can receive. In this situation, the primary benefit is satisfying your own interest.

2. **What would you like to accomplish before you die?** Let's take two examples: Climbing Mount Everest and finding a cure for cancer. What do these different goals say about someone?

- The desire to climb Mount Everest might suggest someone that values travel, adventure, risk, and great, physical challenge.

The desire to find a cure for cancer might mean that person wants to help society, enjoys an intellectual challenge, and prefers to work in solitude rather than in a social setting.

- **What does your dream accomplishment say about you?** Goals that provide a similar reward or require similar types of effort are likely to be a huge turn on for you. Goals that are the opposite are likely to be miserable.

What are you passionate about? Asking yourself that question each night will lead to some interesting answers. Keep track of the responses you receive and write them down.

Notes:

JOURNALING

Habakkuk 2:2
2 Then the LORD answered me and said:
"Write the vision
And make it plain on tablets,
That he may run who reads it.

Believe it or not, I'm not an avid writer. Now don't get me wrong, I have tons of content rolling through my head at any given moment of the day but getting that content out of my head and down on paper is another thing! However, once I learned that the key to retaining information was to write it down, that inspired me to begin to journal. I was kind of afraid in the beginning. Get this, I thought my "thoughts" were not good enough to be journaled. Now how cra-cra does that sound... after all they ARE MY thoughts! Lol! After a while I learned that it was just self-doubt talking.

My thoughts were good enough simply because they belonged to me. They were more or less the story or stories of my life. You too have a story or stories to tell… the pages of your life and or experiences need to be written down. So, I say get writing… you don't have to share your journal with anyone but you. Or on the other hand… you can share them, and they could become the next "Best Seller"! But the key is to write…. write what you feel… think and see. There literally is no right or wrong way to journal and the is NO limit!
~Michelle Aaye

Journaling is a great habit if you want to know more about yourself. Journaling once a week doesn't provide a lot of insight. It's when you do it daily that you can see meaningful results. It's a great activity.

Journaling is:

- Inexpensive. All you need is a pen and paper.
- Revealing. You'll quickly see the patterns in your thinking, life, and behaviors.
- Convenient. You can do it anywhere. A few minutes are all that's required.

Let's Dive In:

Use these strategies to start a journaling habit and learn more about yourself:

1. **Write with a pen and paper rather than using a word processor.** Unless you're physically unable to write, manually writing is best. It's a more complete experience.

2. **Review your day.** What happened that was out of the ordinary? What thoughts do you have about your day? Was it good? Bad? How could it have been better?

3. **Rate how you feel, both mentally and physically, on a scale of 1-10.** Are you tired? Write it down? Do you notice that you've been tired several days in a row? Do something about it. Monitor yourself.

4. **List your successes and failures.** Define your successes and failures. You might want to do this for different areas of your life. For example: work, relationships, goals, and finances.

- **Identifying your successes and failures is the first step to having more successes and fewer failures.**

- Think about what you can do better tomorrow and in the future.

5. **Review your progress.** How are you doing? Reviewing your goals keeps them fresh in your mind.

6. **Write down anything else that seems relevant.** It's your journal, write down whatever you like.

7. **Once every two weeks, read over the previous two weeks.** What are your thoughts about what you read? What insights do you have? How can you use that information?

Keeping a journal can be intimidating. We don't like to look at ourselves too closely. The fact that it makes you uncomfortable is a sign that it would be valuable. There are many signs that you're uncomfortable about it. A few include:

- "I'm too tired."
- "A journal is dumb."
- "This is worthless."
- Any type of excuse to not do it is just your subconscious getting in your way. You know it's a good idea, so just do it.

Writing Prompts

Consider using writing prompts to add to the level of self-discovery. These are just ideas or questions that direct your writing. You can find lists available online. Here are a few to get you started:

- If I had an extra hour each day, how would I spend it?

- What was my favorite job of all time? What did I like about it?

- What do I want my obituary to say about me?

- With unlimited time and money, what career would I pursue if that was the only way I could spend my time?

- What do I need more of in my life? Less?

- How do I believe others would describe me?

Add a writing prompt each day to your regular journaling process. There might not be a better way to learn about yourself.

Notes:

TRAUMA

Joel 2:25-27
25 "So I will restore to you the years that the swarming [a]locust has eaten,
The crawling locust,
The consuming locust,
And the chewing locust,
My great army which I sent among you.
26 You shall eat in plenty and be satisfied,
And praise the name of the LORD your God,
Who has dealt wondrously with you;
And My people shall never be put to shame.
27 Then you shall know that I am in the midst of Israel:
I am the LORD your God
And there is no other.
My people shall never be put to shame.

Trauma?? Its different things to different people. It is something that, if not processed properly, can cause catastrophic results in our lives and the lives of those around us.

I come from an age were dealing with a traumatic incident was handled inside the home and or within the family. That's right, if something BIG happened in the family, you took the issue to "Big Momma" and she was the law and the court system! But you never, EVER took private home matters to a stranger! God forbid that Big Momma couldn't handle your issue... cause if she couldn't, it just wouldn't get handled at all.

This old school philosophy has left hundreds of thousands of women self-medicating and self-curing their own issues the same way Big Momma did. We dealt with trauma by pretending it didn't happen or by pretending we were not affected by it. This method did nothing for the victim but create generational curses that would be passed down through the bloodline from person to person....destroying life after life!

My personal trauma first happened at the age of 21 where I was raped by someone, I thought I could trust. Sadly, this happened to me one other time years later in my 40's; proving that wounds left untreated don't heal they get infected. When I reached out to my mother for help from the first incident I was told to more or less to get over it! And because it was someone, I knew, I was given this phrase as an antidote... "Well Chell, if you lay down with a dog, you'll wake up with fleas, now go on in there and go to bed!"

This was the response I was given... no reassurance that it was not my fault or that it was going to be ok, no talks to understand or process what happened, no love or comfort, just... shame and guilt. I was expected to somehow just "be ok" behind it. Now, I know this seems cold and cruel but when there is a history of rape and sexual abuse in your family and shame has always been the responding answer.... What else would I get?

I survived being rapped twice in my life and I finally and utterly understand at the age of almost 50 that neither time was my fault! And because I did not properly process what happened to me the first time, it left me with gaps and spaces in my comprehension of my rights as a person but more specifically as a woman. I had to gain the knowledge of loving and valuing myself so much so the I stood boldly on the fact that NO MAN has the right to just "have me" against my will!

Be it young or old we HAVE to be able to recognize trauma AND we must recognize how to deal with it PROPERLY. Anyone that knows me knows that I am a big proponent for Therapy/Counseling. The days of keeping trauma a secret are over! We must choose to live healthy lives both physically AND mentally. Yes, dealing with Trauma can be hard but it is a choice we have to make. Left undone, untreated trauma, can literally change the trajectory of your life.

However, you CAN stop the pattern and alter what might have been in your family for years! You CAN win against trauma... because you were absolutely created for so much more!
~Michelle Aaye

If you or someone you love is dealing with untreated sexual trauma and need help, contact RAINN(Rape, Abuse & Incest National Network) 1-800-656-HOPE. Make the call and get help!

Trauma, especially in childhood, can have a huge impact on your thoughts and behavior later in life. It doesn't matter if the cause of the trauma seems silly as an adult. The fact that it was traumatic at the time is what's important.

Being afraid of a bully or losing a beloved pet in first grade might seem inconsequential today, but it wasn't then. It had an impact.

Of course, bigger things like abuse or losing a parent can have even bigger consequences.

Let's Dive In:

Answer these questions to discover the negative events from your past that may be influencing you today:

1. **What are your worst memories from your childhood?** How did those impact you? How did they change you? Did it change the choices you made at that time? Later in life?

2. **What would you tell yourself if you could go back in time?** Imagine that your adult self is talking to your younger self. What would you say? What advice would you give regarding that negative event?

3. **Does it still impact you?** Do you view the world in a certain way because of those events? Do those events change how you make decisions?

4. **Ask the same questions for events that happened after childhood.** Include bad relationships, negative events associated with work, and anything else that's happened since you turned 18.

Some people are able to shake off negative experiences with few long-lasting effects. Some of us are affected by traumatic events much more profoundly. Our brains are so intent on protecting us that our responses to trauma can be extreme.

Understand the traumatic events from your past and how they have impacted your life. Notice if they are still impacting your life.

Are they responsible for the limitations you put on yourself? Do they affect your relationships with other people? Are your values impacted by the traumatic events you've experienced?

Do you agree with these limitations? If not, how can you go about changing them?

Notes:

FINAL TIPS

A few final tips for the committed. There are plenty of things you can do here and there to increase your awareness of yourself. These are interesting activities you might not think of on your own. On the other hand, with a little effort, you might find even better ideas!

Let's Dive In:

Here are 9 more ways to learn more about yourself:

1. **Take a long walk by yourself in nature.** What kind of things did you think about? What did you notice about your thoughts? A more serious version of this is to go camping by yourself for a long weekend. Find a remote spot.

2. **Read a book about something that makes you upset.** Maybe you're a diehard Christian. Read a book about Judaism or Satanism. Perhaps a book written by a white supremacist would really get under your skin. Read a book you don't agree with and notice your response.

3. **Make a video of yourself talking to a friend or stranger.** You'll either need to be sneaky or you'll need some help. How do you appear to others? We can't watch ourselves interact with others without recording ourselves.

    - Watch your body language. How is what you're seeing and hearing different from the perception you had before seeing and hearing yourself?

4. **Go on a meditation retreat.** Meditate for 10 or more days straight. You'll find out more than you could ever imagine.

5. **Ask yourself "why" until you get an answer you can use:**

    - Why do I hate parties? Because I can't talk to strangers.

    - Why can't I talk to strangers? Because it makes me nervous.

    - Why does it make me nervous? Because I don't know what to say.

    - Why don't I know what to say? Because I don't have anything planned in advance.

- Try this exercise and see what you find out.

6. **Write a personal manifesto.** What do you want your life to represent? What is your credo? What are your rules for life?

7. **Take online personality tests.** Some of these online tests are more credible than others. The best tests will often have a small fee, but the price is worth the information.

8. **Ask yourself, "Who am I?"** Keep asking yourself. Ask hundreds of times over the course of several weeks. Keep asking and notice the answers you receive.

9. **List your 10 biggest regrets.** These are things you've done or failed to do. Why do you regret them?

CONCLUSION

John 15:5
"I am the vine; you are the branches. If you remain in me and I in you, you will bear much fruit; apart from me you can do nothing.

Knowing yourself is a challenging task. Ask yourself these final questions to align your perspective of who you are to who God created you to be.

Who is God in relation to me?
John 15:5-"I am the vine; you are the branches. If you remain in me and I in you, you will bear much fruit; apart from me you can do nothing.

Who am I?
Genesis 1:27-So God created man in His *own* image; in the image of God, He created him; male and female He created them.

2 Corinthians 5:17-Therefore, if anyone *is* in Christ, *he is* a new creation; old things have passed away; behold, all things have become new.
Ephesians 2:10-For we are His workmanship, created in Christ Jesus for good works, which God prepared beforehand that we should walk in them.
2 Corinthians 5:21-For He made Him who knew no sin *to be* sin for us, that we might become the righteousness of God in Him.

Whose Am I?
1 John 3:1- Behold what manner of love the Father has bestowed on us, that we should be called children of [a]God! Therefore the world does not know us, because it did not know Him.

Finally...

You've spent every second of your life with yourself. You've been there for every experience. Yet, you often have more insight into someone you know at a casual level than you do into yourself.

We are composed of our values, experiences, habits, and preferences. The mistakes we repeat limit us. Due to this our passions remain hidden.

We're so busy worrying about the opinions of people that we don't even care that we don't know ourselves anymore.

In the end, the ONLY real way to know yourself is to find out who God is. Take some time to learn about "WHO" He is and "Why" He created you.

Once you discover the love God has for you, then you can love and know your *true* self! Self-love is the most important part of knowing who you are and who you are to become.

Knowing your true self is a fundamental key to success. Without self-knowledge, luck has a great influence over the results in life. The results in your life should be based your intentions not accidental happenstance.

Our true self is that part of us that never changes.

We often cover up the true self with false beliefs and fears. We superimpose the desires of society over our own. So, finding the true self requires that we go back to the beginning. Back to where God first loved us!

Spend more time with God so that getting to know your true self is easier. Once you do, you can finally soar!

RESOURCES

Women's Personal Development/
Mentoring
Michelle Aaye
www.michelleaaye.com
Michelle Aaye- Facebook

Life Coaching
Melissa Wilson
In2Me Life Coaching

Trauma Services
RAINN
(Rape, Abuse & Incest National Network)
1-800-656-HOPE

Women's Shelter Services (St. Louis)

Pregnant Women's Shelter Services (St. Louis)
Hope House

AAYE Ladies.... Thank You so much for choosing to begin your personal journey to self with me! Remember loving others begins with loving yourself!

God Bless!
Michelle Aaye

www.ingramcontent.com/pod-product-compliance
Lightning Source LLC
Chambersburg PA
CBHW071103090426
42737CB00013B/2448
* 9 7 8 1 7 3 7 4 6 3 7 0 2 *